How to Analyze People

The Ultimate Guide to Human Psychology, Body Language, Personality Types, and Reading People

Table of Contents

Introduction

What is the one most important skill that you would like to pick up to succeed personally and professionally in today's world? Considering a majority of our personal, professional and social life is determined by interacting and developing relationships or connections with other people. Analyzing people, indeed, is the most premium success skill to acquire.

How do you determine if a potential employee will be a good fit for your organization? How do you gauge if the hot new date you fancy will also be an encouraging and supportive long-term partner? How do you negotiate to win some deals with strangers you know little about? How do you network at social or business gatherings to form mutually beneficial associations? How do you build a killer rapport with existing clients such that they only want to work with you?

The key to all this lays in analyzing people and understanding their personality, behavior, thoughts, and feelings.

What is it that drives these people? What does their body language subconsciously reflect about their thoughts and feelings? What is their fundamental personality? When you learn to read people and understand their basic personality and thought patterns, you mold your communication pattern to suit it, thus making the interaction more effective.

When you can read or predict someone's behavior, you are in a position to model your own behavior or actions to develop a solid rapport with the person, thus leading to more rewarding relationships/associations. I am not training you to be an FBI agent (well, you may get even better than the sleuths).

Learning to read people is one of the sharpest skills you can pick up in today's world. It will give you the power to deliver your message exactly as intended, thus minimizing the scope of misunderstanding. You'll be more in control of a conversation, be a better negotiator, a more empathetic friend, or a supportive leader. There will be lesser conflict situations, and you'll develop greater understanding towards other people's shortcomings.

Your ability to read people deeply influences the quality of your relationships. When you learn the tricks and techniques of analyzing people, you know exactly what clues you should be looking for while trying to understand people. How does their body language reveal what they leave unsaid? What does their choice of words speak about their personality and character? What personality type do they belong to? How to spot deception?

Glossy magazines does a great disservice to the pursuit of analyzing people by reducing it to a bunch of pop quizzes such as "What Your Man/Woman's Favorite Food Says About Him or Her" or "What's Your Favorite Fragrance Says About You." Analyzing people can be entertaining,but it's not as non-serious, frivolous or trivial study as it's made out to be by various smartphone apps and magazines. To be a near accurate people reader, you need lots of practice and serious attempts at decoding people's personalities. Much as you'd like to believe, you can't reveal much about people through the color of their eyes.

Though the subject has volumes and volumes of research devoted to it, I am bringing to the most proven, actionable, concise and effective people reading techniques that you can benefit from with consistent practice and effort. These can be used everywhere from interpersonal relationships to your professional life to social circles. When you know exactly what to look for while reading people, the sky is really limit to where it can lead you.

Did you know that the ability to read a person's body language can help you predict the outcome of any negotiation accurately about 80 percent of the time? Now that's definitely an edge!

Human beings are wired through primitive times (and this is one thing evolution has left untouched) to communicate with one another through subconscious signals. Even though a person may not vocalize his/her feelings of being upset with you, their body language will convey the disappointment and resentment at a subconscious level. When you consciously learn to decode these clues, you are better able to reach out to the person and communicate effectively. What is gut feeling or instinct? It is nothing but you latching on to certain clues a person is emitting at a more subconscious level.

Notice how when someone smiles or yawns, your smile and yawn muscles are involuntarily activated at a subconscious level. Our brains are wired to catch clues that are not captured by the conscious mind. For example, when a person is fuming from within and pretending to be pleasant on the surface, don't we experience a strange, almost instinctive feeling that something is wrong? He or she doesn't appear angry on the surface,but their body language reveals discomfort in the form of a faster heartbeat or higher blood pressure. We catch this at a subconscious level that gives us the "something isn't what it seems" feeling.

Tracking man's evolutionary patterns will lead you to the insight that our cognitive minds were always capable of making accurate conclusions about another person's thoughts and feelings. How do you think early humans communicated in the absence of spoken or written language? It was only through body language, tone, expressions and other similar mechanisms. This means the ability to read people is inherently present in us. We just need to sharpen and develop the ability to tune in to it at a more conscious level to form more fulfilling and rewarding relationships.

Everyone from salespersons to trial attorneys use the art of reading people to their advantage. I know some car salespersons who are trained to peep into the cars of their prospective customers to analyze them and make interesting small talk. For instance, if they find a golf kit at the back of the car, they'll start the conversation with how they love to play golf on weekends just to develop a rapport with the potential customer based on mutual hobbies.

Similarly, trial attorneys try to decipher which way the jury is swinging when jurors glance in the direction of the witnesses or accused/defendant or the body language of the judge when the opposing attorney is cross-examining a witness. Similarly, clients are also briefed about keeping their body language compatible with the general impression they are trying to convey to the jurors and the public. This can mean eliminating all behavior that points to deception, such as no fidgeting, avoiding darting eye movements across the room and other similar patterns.

When you learn to read people accurately, it helps you see them in a less judgmental light. You also learn to observe misleading and deceitful behavior. Think of a situation where a falsely flatters you to win favors. When you know how to read people, you can differentiate between genuine compliments and false flattery, while protecting your own interests. Once you master the art of reading people, it is easy to call out deception.

Here are some benefits of being an amazing people reader.

> Reading people saves you the time and effort of dealing only with people who are ethical and match your expectations, weeding out all the energy draining folks. You don't have to kiss a million frogs to discover your prince.

- More fulfilling, gratifying and rewarding interpersonal relationships, minimizing the heartache of broken relationships.

- Hiring the most suitable employees for your organization.

- The ability to tell when people are deceitful, from calling out your partner's lies in a relationship to knowing when potential employees are not honest during interviews.

- The ability to read people helps us select a long-term partner who matches our own personality, behavior characteristics, attitude, values, and goals. It also helps identify if a person is attracted to you, which can be used to pursue the relationship further.

- Analyzing people make you a more effective leader at work. When you understand what drives your team (along with their thoughts, goals,and feelings), it is easier to get them to be more motivated and productive. There will be greater overall efficiency and job satisfaction. This single most important trait (the ability to understand and connect with people) can be your elevator to corporate success.

- ➢ -Negotiations and sales targets are easier to achieve. When you understand how a potential customer or client/business associate is thinking, it easier to steer the direction of the negotiation in your favor. It will help you recognize if people are genuinely interested in your current offer or if they need a better offer or more time to think. You can quickly gauge people's interest and apprehensions. For instance, if you quote a price and the other party verbally says they'd like a better price but their body language and other non-verbal signals convey that they are elated with the current price (or that they are sold), you won't bargain or negotiate any further.

> Learning to analyze people is a great way to mold your own verbal and nonverbal communication for leaving a stunning first impression on people. It will help you rebrand and repackage your personality to form more beneficial relationships/associations. You know how to come as more honest, credible, likable and authoritative according to the demands of the situation by sending the appropriate clues.

➢ You'll be able to be a more empathetic person and reach out to people in times of distress to form better interpersonal relationships.

➢ Reading people will allow you to come out tops in job interviews by conveying the right body language in the presence of recruiters. You will know how to build the perfect impression by subtly conveying the values/ideas suitable for the position. In short, you'll know how to demonstrate through clues that you are a perfect fit for the role and organization.

➢ You'll be an exceptional speaker and communicator when you tune in to the body language of your audience. As a people reader, it is easier to understand when you are saying things that strikes the right chord with people, and when they're amused or moved by something.

You can adjust your speech to make it more interesting/appealing to your audience. It helps you relate to them and make your points more persuasively or convincingly. Reading your audience or potential customer helps you establish a common ground for better results.

➢ You will be able to select the right leaders and influencers based on their verbal and nonverbal clues and personality types. Learn to look for traits such as power, authority, empathy, integrity and other characteristics of a leader. The ability to observe their body language will help you decipher if they are simply power hungry or genuinely cares about the betterment of their people.

Chapter One: Secrets of Decoding Body Language

Have you ever wondered by people insist on meeting someone face to face while discussing important matters? Why are job candidates generally not interviewed over the phone? It is undoubtedly this need to read clues people leave unsaid that makes the communication more effective.

Research has pointed to the fact that about 80 percent of our communication happens through nonverbal channels, which makes reading body language and other nonverbal clues so important while analyzing people.

Here are some of the most proven and effective tips for analyzing a person's body language.

Face and Head

A person's face and head can reveal plenty about their thoughts and feelings because it is one of the most noticeable parts of our body. This is also the region that is giving out verbal clues, which makes it an unbeatable combination while reading people near accurately.

A slightly tilted or slanted head can indicate interesting or attention. It can also be a sign of empathy towards the listener. When people are genuinely interested in what you are speaking or are listening to you in an empathetic manner, they will most likely lean their head in your direction.

Similarly, when you grab someone's interest or attention, their eyes will be wider than normal. Nope, not as much as these over the top sitcoms would have you believe but a little wider than normal.

Direct and unshifting eye contact is more or less a sign of integrity, honestyhighconfidence, interest, and courage. People who aren't speaking the truth or are dishonest by disposition often shift their gaze or rarely hold continuous eye contact. It is alright too if people move away their gaze every once in a while. However, a person who is constantly avoiding eye contact may not be trustworthy.

Even the direction in which our eye moves reveals a lot about us.

Our eye movements are closely connected to specific regions of the brain. Hence when the brain performs specific functions, it stimulates the eyes to move in a specific direction.

When a person is asked for precise information that is stored in the memory, he/she will move their eyes to the upper left. On the other hand, when a person is making up information or stories, their eyes will move to the upper right. They are not recalling information from memory but making it up. The reverse is true for left-handed people. When their eyes move to the upper right, they recall information, whereas if their eyes move to the upper left, they are constructing information.

When there's an internal conflict going on in a person (choosing between two options for instance), their eyes will move towards the left collarbone. This signifies an inner dialogue (for instance when a person is caught between lying and uttering the truth). Excessive lateral eye movements (from one side to another) can also signify deception.

When people try to recall sounds, their eyes dart in the lateral right side. Similarly, when a person tries to recall a specific sensation, their eyes will move in the lower right direction. When a person is making up a conversation he or she didn't have, their eyes almost always move in the left lateral side. They are simply making up the sound or conversation that never happened.

Expanded pupils or excessive blinking are an indicator of attraction or lust. It is also a sign that the person is deeply interested in what you are speaking. If a person looks you upwards to downwards (and maybe upwards again), they are seizing you a prospective sexual partner or enemy. It can also be an indicator of dominance and intimidation.

Beware of making sweeping judgments about people simply based on their eye movements and look for a group of clues that point to a single direction because external stimuli such as light and sound can impact eye movements.

If a person is genuinely smiling, their smile will impact their eyes. It will create wrinkled skin and crow's feet at the corner of the person's eyes. Conversely, fake smiles will only affect the mouth corners without slightly crinkling the skin around our eyes.

Learn to observe micro-expressions (the natural result of voluntary and involuntary responses that conflict with each other) that happen in microseconds. They are so instinctive and involuntary that it is almost impossible to manipulate these expressions. For instance, when a person lies, their mouth will slant slightly for a fraction of a second or the eyes will roll slightly. Eye movements discussed earlier are also a component of microexpressions.

Hand Gestures

Notice how people who are extremely demonstrative and expressive in nature talk through gestures, which offer a window into what they are thinking and feeling. Arms that are wide open indicate a feeling of being relaxed, at ease, flexible and upbeat about novel ideas. These folks are not afraid to experiment with new ideas or enjoy new experiences.

Conversely, crossing arms is a sign of being rigid, inflexible, disinterested or closed. If a person is sitting across you with their arms crossed he or she likely doesn't accept your ideas or is not interested in them. It can also point to suspicion on their part. They are subconsciously closing themselves from the conversation through the act of creating a symbolic barrier. The person could also be acting defensive or may not be too comfortable with the conversation.

Running fingers through the hair is a typical gesture of being uncertain or thinking what to speak next. The person is buying time to determine his or her subsequent move.

Similarly, rubbing the brow is a sign of anxiety or uncertainty.

When a person covers their mouth while you are talking they most likely do not believe what you are saying. Similarly, if a person uses this gesture while talking, it may not be wise to trust their words. It's a subconscious act where they are stopping themselves from speaking the truth.

If a person is stroking his or her chin, it may be a sign of deep thinking.

Notice how people are constantly touching their earlobe during an interaction. It is a sign that he or she is seeking comfort since that is one of the body's most sensitive parts.

The palm up gesture is widely used to reveal openness and transparency. It is seen as non-threatening, friendly and submissive. On the other hand, the palm down gesture can reveal power, dominance, authority, forcefulness, and aggression. Wasn't this Hitler's trademark salute?

Forming a steeple with both the hands may most likely indicate that the person is in a position of authority or self-confident by nature. It can also be used by people who want to show that they are in control or power.

Clenched hands reveal anxiety, frustration, stress, and restraint. Similarly, hands in the pocket gesture is formed when the person has a more closed attitude and wishes to keep to himself or herself. If it's only the left hand that's in the pocket, he/she is concealing something related to feelings and/or interpersonal relationships.

Legs

Even though the legs and feet are probably the least noticed part of the human body during communication, it can tell a lot about a person's feelings and thoughts. Since people almost never look at their legs, people do not usually manipulate or control their leg movements as much as say eye contact or facial expressions.

Feet pointed in your direction during communication reveals attention, affiliation, trust, interest and a connection. There is a high chance the person subconsciously thinking in the same direction as you.

On the contrary, if a person's feet are pointed in the opposite direction, or they assume one-foot-out position, he or she is most likely not interested or in agreement with what you are saying. Subconsciously, they are looking for an escape route.

Crossed legs, much like crossed arms, are a sign of being disinterested, disbelieving or inflexible. It indicates that the person isn't very receptive to your ideas. You may need to inspire their trust by building a rapport or convince them further using another technique.

This posture is often assumed by people when they are listening to a business idea or listening to a sales pitch. If you spot the person assuming a cross-legged gesture, quickly change the topic and get them into a more open subconscious mind before getting back to the original conversation.

Transferring weight from one leg to another can be an indicator of anxiety, nervousness, stress, disinterest or discomfort. When a person is lying, he/she makes excessive foot movements to avoid stress or escape. Tapping feet is also a sign of nervousness or boredom.

Voice Tone

A person's tone can speak volumes about what he/she is thinking or feeling. If you observe several inconsistencies in the person's tone, they may be more excited, angry, stressed or nervous than usual. It can also be an indication of hiding important information or lying. On the other hand, the volume of a person's voice while speaking can also be revealing. If they are speaking in a tone that is softer and slower than usual, something may be amiss.

A person's tone can add several layers to the communication to make it more impactful, while also lending more meaning to what they are conveying. For instance, when a person says "you are looking really nice today" in a sarcastic tone with emphasis on "today," you know they mean you don't usually look this nice everyday and that they are surprised that you can actually look this good! Even though the person has offered you a compliment on the face of it, their tone and emphasis help you read between the lines.

The meaning of a sentence changes entirely when you change the tone or inflection. For example, if a person says, "She stole the ring" in a flat tone, he/she is making a statement definitively accusing someone. Similarly, if the tone is slightly raised towards the end, they are questioning or raising a doubt about the accusation. The words used are the exactly the same, but the intonation awards it an altogether different meaning. When someone speaks in a flat tone than raising tone often, they may have a more authoritative and assertive personality.

Similarly, emphasizing on different words can also alter the meaning of a sentence. For example, a sentence like, "Did you steal the book?" can have several different meanings when the emphasis changes. If the person emphasizes in the book, they may mean, did you steal the book or something else. Similarly, if the emphasis is on you, it may imply did you do it or was it done by someone else. Again, emphasizing on steal would mean, did you steal it or simply borrow it with the intention of return it. There, emphasizing on three different words has given us three distinct meanings.

Make Your Reading More Effective

Here are some valuable pointers for making your body language reading even more effective.

Look For a Group of Clues

The biggest blunder people make while analyzing body language is to make sweeping, inaccurate conclusions based on a few isolated clues. Instead, if you want to make your predictions more comprehensive, look at a cluster of clues together. For instance, if you spot a person making excessive leg movements or sweating conclude he or she is lying when they may be nervous; you end up doing an incorrect reading. Similarly, a person may shift their weight from one side to other because the seat is uncomfortable.

You need to watch out for clues originating from different parts of the body to make the reading more comprehensive and accurate rather than looking at standalone clues. Another example, someone who is lying may simply maintain consistent eye contact to mislead you into believing them. If you make a sweeping conclusion based only on the eye contact, you read the person incorrectly. If you look at other clues such as sweaty palms, shifting feet, nose rubbing, feet pointed towards the exit and others, you can collectively conclude they are lying.

Establish a Baseline

Set a clear baseline for analyzing a person. You may not always have the opportunity to do that, but it sets the tone for a more accurate reading while offering more in-depth insights into his or her personality.

How does the person normally react in a given situation? If he or she is a quick thinking, energetic, passionate and always charged up individual, he/she will be fidgeting all the time. They'll want to do something all time, which can be misread as clues (tapping fingers, shifting from one leg to another, bouncing feet) of nervousness or deceit.

Understand a person's primary nature before attempting to read them. How is their regular speech and voice tone? How do they usually express emotions such as happiness, excitement, nervousness, enthusiasm and more? This will help you read them more efficiently and eliminate fallacies. When you notice the inconsistency in their regular behavior or a mismatch between verbal and nonverbal communication, you know something isn't quite what it appears.

Setting

Sometimes the setting also influences a person's behavior. For instance, the same person's body language will be different at work (more formal, restrained and rigid) with co-workers than when he or she is socializing with them over the weekend (more casual, comfortable, gregarious and flexible) over the weekend.

Similarly, a person who is otherwise confident and self-assured may show signs of nervousness during a job interview. It is the setting or situation causes a shift in the person's behavior. For all you know, a person may cross their arms and legs because they are feeling cold or they may lean in the opposite direction because the seating isn't very comfortable. This is precisely why you should be looking at a cluster of signals rather than relying on a single clue.

Cultures

The same gestures, movements, and expressions can have different connotations in different cultures. While some gestures like a smile are more universal, others should be read in a cultural context when you are dealing with people from different cultures. Avoid the mistake of reading some clues using your cultural filter. Just like behavior, establish a baseline for the culture a person originates from.

For instance, Italians are known to be very expressive, vivacious and gregarious in their communication. They gesticulate enthusiastically. On the other hand, someone from England will behave in a more restrained, stoic and reserved manner.

Again, a single gesture can have different interpretations in different cultures.

Though a thumbs-up sign is symbolic of wishing someone good luck in western nations, it is viewed as rude in some regions within the Middle East. People from the western countries like to keep some physical distance while interacting with someone for the first time, which is symbolic of guarding their privacy or personal space. Not understanding these cultural differences may prove expensive when you are dealing with global business associates.

Chapter Two: Psychological Theories for Analyzing People

Psychological theories attempt to reveal what shapes people's personalities and why they behave the way they do. Every theory emphasizes on different aspects of the individual to understand the fundamental question of why he or she behaves, thinks, acts or feels in a particular way. It offers a framework to study a person's personality, behavior,and actions.

Here are the top psychological theories used for analyzing people.

Biological

The biological theory focuses on pinning down human behavior to the influence of a person's genetics. The basic premise of the biological, psychological theory is that a human being's behavior and thought process can be effectively explained by gaining insights into their anatomy, evolution, genetics and physiological development. The emphasis is on our brain and central nervous system.

Behaviorism

Behaviorism focuses on the impact of prior learning experiences on an individual's personality. Behaviorists do not emphasize the importance of mental or cognitive forces in shaping a person's behavior. In their opinion, the mind is too complex a tool to decode or objectively analyze. This theory focuses on the premise that our behavior or personality is a reflection of our learning and experiences.

For instance, it has been concluded that exposing children to violent television shows and video games build violent tendencies in them. According to behaviorism, we are a sum of our learning and experiences.

If a child turns out to be a bullying, aggressive and angry adult, he/she may have had a violent or aggressive childhood or grown up in a home where violence was prevalent. Similarly, if a person always craves attention and acceptance from others, he/she may have grown up facing rejection from their parents or with the feeling that they are never able to meet their parents' acceptance.

Similarly, when a home is filled with books and high emphasis is placed by well-educated parents on reading, seeking knowledge and cognitive development, the person is likelier to excel in academics and grow up to be a highly educated and successful professional.

This psychological and people analyzing theory says that a majority of dominant behavior patterns can be pinned down to early childhood experiences.

Sociocultural Theory

Sociocultural theory emphasizes on social and cultural factors impacting a person's behavior. Trends such as tattoos in the 90s are a fine example of the influence of sociocultural factors. For instance, before the 90s, people with tattoos were seen as punks. Post the tattoo phenomenon of the 90s, it became an accepted cultural trend.

The essence of the sociocultural theory is that an individual's behavior, development or personality is a direct result of what he/she gains through his /her societal influences. It can be in the form of cultural symbols, language,and traditions. These are the factors, which, according to sociocultural theorists, shape an individual's overall personality.

For instance, someone who grows up in a crime infested area with druggies and dropouts is likelier to take to crime as an accepted way of life owing to their social influences. He or she is exposed to the social culture of using force and earning money/fame through unlawful means, which has shaped his/her behavior in a similar direction. They may display traits of aggression, violence, and force.

Socio-cultural psychologists are of the view that a person's development and personality can never be examined in isolation of his/her social environment. They believe that a person's development occurs in an essentially social context, which implies we are products of our immediate cultural and social influences. For instance, if a person is born in a more creative culture and social set-up where new ideas and thinking out of the box is encouraged, he or she will develop the same inventive and creative thought process.

Psychoanalytical

Psychoanalysis focuses on the impact of unconscious mental forces and early childhood development such as impulses, childhood wishes, childish desires and reality demands. The theory was put forth by Sigmund Freud and has become one of the most popular theories for analyzing an individual's personality.

According to Freud's theory, all our behavior is a result of the interaction between the id, ego,and superego. It is the conflict and relationship between these three elements that determine or impacts our behavior. He held the view that the human personality is a result of a series of psychosexual phases. Each phase represents a conflict between the human biological desires and expectations of the society within which he/she lives. This conflict ultimately impacts human behavior.

Trait Theory

The trait theory is one of the most important personality analysis theories in modern psychology. According to this theory, an individual's personality comprises a cluster of broad traits that cause the person to act and behave in a particular manner. Eysenck's three dimension theory is one of the most widely used trait theories.

The psychologist concluded that there are three fundamental personality dimensions (psychoticism, extroversion, and neuroticism), and the personality of an individual is determined by the combination of varying levels of these traits in people. Another set of modern researchers mentioned five broad traits that made up an individual's personality. The five personality traits were identified as extroversion, openness, neuroticism, agreeableness, and conscientiousness.

Extraverts are sociable creatures who desire constant change, energy,and excitement. They are more carefree, impulsive, spontaneous and optimistic. These are the adventure and thrill seekers. Eysenck concluded that because extraverts have a partially aroused nervous system, they are constantly seeking stimulation to restore an optimum level of stimulation. Conversely, introverts are on the other side of the scale. They have an over-stimulated nervous system and avoid further sensation.

Chapter Three: The 8 Types of Introverts

The Myers-Briggs Type Indicator categorizes everyone into 16 distinct types of personalities, elaborating on Carl Jung's introvert and extrovert classification of personality. All of us exhibit varied preferences in our interactions with people around us, and this according to the Carl Jung and Myers-Briggs Type indicates our personality.

In the Myers Briggs, introverts and extroverts are further divided into 8 different personality types, each based on their intuition, sensing, thinking, judging, feeling and perceiving. Three of these six elements along with their basic introvert or extrovert personality are what determine their overall personality. The Myers-Briggs personality assessment test can be taken online to determine your or another person's personality type.

Here are the 8 different types of introverts as classified by the widely followed Myers-Briggs Type Indicator.

Introverts predominantly prefer spending time by themselves while contemplating and reflecting upon options or ideas before taking clear action. They tend to be happiest when they can make a decision, and instantly take to ideas rather than the actual implementation of these ideas.

Intuition or Sensing (N or S)

The first letter in the Myers-Briggs personality type indicates whether the person is an introvert or extrovert. The second letter or category symbolizes the manner through which they see the world. While people driven by intuition will listen to their inner voice, those driven by sensing will reply more on the outside world for information.

Thinking or Feeling (T or F)

The third category or letter in the Myers-Briggs personality indicator symbolizes the way through which the person processes information or facts. Thinking people are high on logic and rationale, and their decisions are primarily driven by logical analysis. Conversely, feeling folks' decisions are more influenced by inner feelings and emotions.

Perceiving or Judging (P or J)

Judging or perceiving is the last letter defining an individual's personality in the four-letter Myers-Briggs personality indicator. How does the person use the knowledge that is in his or her possession is what defines this category. Judging people gather experiences and knowledge and fiercely stick to their views.

Conversely, perceiving folks are known to look at multiple possibilities before developing their stance.

Variations of these eight letters combine to create 16 personality types, where the first letter is the fundamental or basic personality (Introvert or Extrovert). The second letter symbolizes if an individual is an intuitive and sensing type of person, while the third letter presents if they are primarily driven by logic or feelings. The fourth or final letter represents whether they are the information judging or perceiving type.

ISTJ

Introverted, Sensing, Thinking, Judging

ISTJs are serious and contemplative by nature who prefer a secure, quiet and peaceful living. Their behavior is marked by the need to be dependable, responsible and perfectionists. They are logical, analytical and practical by nature while working towards their goals with a single-minded dedication. ISTJs also have deep respect for establishments, authority,and tradition. They don't believe in going off the beaten path and would rather keep order or organization in their personal and professional lives.

ISFJ

Introverted, Sensing, Feeling, Judging

ISFJs are reserved, conscientious and compassionate. They have a deep sense of responsibility and obligations towards meeting their commitments. There is a high need to place the needs of others before theirs. Again, the ISFJs are practical and steady by nature, along with the possessing respect for security, established customs and traditions. Their inner world is very varied and rich, and they are very sensitive when it comes tuning in to other people's feelings. Serving others is a way of life for them, and they actively look for opportunities to be of help to others.

INFJ

Introvert, Intuitive, Feeling, Judging

INFJs are reticent, forceful, sensitive and fiercely original. There are forever looking for connections between ideas, material possessions,and humans. There is also a tendency to be inquisitive about motives and insights behind people's behavior patterns. INFJs are committed to their values and deeply conscientious by nature. They possess a clear view of things and know how to come to a resolution that is in the best interests of everyone involved. They are organized, clear and decisive when it comes to making a decision, and know how to implement ideas that are good for everyone.

INTJ

Introvert, Intuitive, Thinking, Judging

INTJs are original, fiercely independent, determined, rational and analytical by nature. They have a natural flair for converting intangible theories into practical action. They also have the tendency to spot in clear pattern in events and are also able to articulately explain them in a detailed manner. They are committed to their roles and will almost always take a task to its logical conclusion, without giving up midway despite challenges. They set very high standards for their performance and have huge expectations when it comes to other people's performance too. INTJs make for good leaders (and followers too if the leader inspires their trust).

ISTP

Introvert, Sensing, Thinking, Perceiving

ISTPs are quiet, contemplative, reserved and deeply curious about the manner in which things work. They possess amazing mechanical skills and show an inclination towards adventure sports. ISTPs are tolerant and patient and will observe things peacefully until they can come up with a clear solution. They are deeply interested in the cause and effect relationship between things and organize facts according to clear principles. ISTPs are excellent when it comes to seeking practical solutions for problems, though they may come across as slightly detached or increasingly rational.

ISFP

Introverted, Sensing, Feeling, Perceiving

ISFPs are reserved, reticent, compassionate, sensitive and serious. They hate conflict and confrontation of any kind and steer away from activities that are bound to create conflict. ISFPs are known for their loyalty and faithfulness while demonstrating a huge inclination for aesthetics. They are open-minded, adaptable, flexible, while also being fiercely original and creative in their approach. The ISFP personality type loves their personal space, and work with their own set of rules and principles at their pace. They are extremely mindful of the present moment and appreciate the now rather than living in the past or future.

INFP

Introverted, Intuitive, Feeling, Perceiving

These are quiet, idealistic, contemplative and reflective people. They have a deep sense of loyalty towards their principles and people they value. Their value system is highly developed,and INFPs will seldom go against their values. They are idealistic who aim to live according to their values. INFP personality type people are adaptable, flexible and laid-back (only until their values aren't challenged). They have a deep interest in helping others.

INTP

Introverted, Intuitive, Thinking, and Perceiving

INTPs are analytical, independent thinking, logical and deeply original by nature. They are driven by theories, logic,and ideas. INTP personality type values knowledge, skills,and competency. They are reticent, reserved and not easy to understand. They are fiercely individualistic and don't care much about being a leader or follower. INTPs believe in creating their own space and rules.

Chapter Four: The 8 Types of Extroverts

Similar to the previous chapter, there are eight types of extroverts in the Myers-Briggs Personality Indicator. Here is a detailed breakdown of each.

Extroverted people are driven by a desire to be actively engaged in events and activities that involve plenty of social interaction. They enjoy being with other people and are at home within large groups. Extroverts tend to enjoy energizing and getting others into action. They are likelier to cope with challenging situations by talking through then rather than internally reflecting upon these issues.

ESTP

Extrovert, Sensing, Thinking, Perceiving

ESTPs shoot straight without beating around the bush and like to a take a more logical, and practical approach to life. They steer towards practical solutions that provide immediate solutions in challenging situations. The ESTP personality type is gifted with the ability to pick up signals of other people's feelings and personality, which sharpens their social skills. They are wary of intangible theories and prefer action and implementation over abstract theories. This personality type is spontaneous and learns by doing rather than seeing. They also tend to enjoy and live in the present.

ESFP

Extrovert, Sensing, Feeling, and Perceiving

ESFP personality type people believe the world is full of possibilities, positive people,and novel experiences. They are gregarious, outgoing, accommodating and friendly. The often find themselves excelling in the role of a negotiator, diplomat or peacemaker since they are affable by nature. ESFPs are also optimistic and spontaneous. They enjoy working in teams and making the impossible possible by combining their strengths with those of others. During stressful situations, they find it tough to cope with negative possibilities. They enjoy life and their connections with others.

ENFP

Extroverted, Intuitive, Feeling, Perceiving

These are warm, positive and enthusiastic people, who are full of bright ideas and the potential to fulfill them. There is no limit to possibilities according to the ENFP personality type. They have a wide range of interests and perform well while doing what they are passionate about. The ENFP type can establish quick and logical links between events. They have complete confidence in moving ahead based on their perceptions. When negative, they can be highly manipulative or use their glib tongue for deceitful purposes.

ENTP

Extroverted, Intuitive, Thinking, Perceiving

ENTP is high on ideas and intuition. They can understand and tune in to people's emotions almost instantly. The ENTP tribe is spontaneous, alert and frank. They won't hesitate to call a spade a spade. They are keen on developing new ideas. They rely on different possibilities rather than a single plan of action. ENTPs are great conversationalists and tend to enjoy lively, interesting conversations and arguments. ENTP type people are good at analyzing people, and nothing bores them more than a set routine. They respect knowledge, wisdom,and possibilities.

ESTJ

Extroverted, Sensing, Thinking, Judging

ESTJs cherish the present moment, and respect traditions and established rules. They have very clear beliefs and codes of living. The ESTJ personality type is practical, forthright and logical by nature. They tend to take charge of any situation, and a have a good grip on how things should be executed. They seamlessly step into leadership roles and do well at organizing people and tasks in a detailed manner. Once they take on a task, they give it all they have. They value stability and order. During stressful situations, they alienated from others.

ESFJ

Extroverted, Sensing, Feeling and Judging

ESFJ people take a deep interest in other people. They have a strong interest to be loved by everyone, and work towards making any situation pleasant. This makes others rely on them for support and positivity. The ESFJ personality type possesses the innate ability to make people feel great about themselves. ESFJs are warm, co-operative, supportive and conscientious. Their values are more defined by people and community rather than internally. ESFJ people enjoy appreciation and contributing to the community.

ENFJ

Extroverted, Sensing, Feeling, Judging

The sky is the limit for ENFJ people, and their world is brimming with possibilities. They possess exceptional people skills and are affectionate, responsible and empathetic towards people. They are outwardly focused and don't fancy spending alone time (it drives them into negative thinking). The ENFJ personality type can easily spot the talent in others and are always keen to help others achieve their true potential or calling. They always tend to keep a part of themselves hidden, even in a group. ENFJs respond well to both appreciation and criticism and are known to be faithful.

ENTJ

Extroverted, Intuitive, Thinking, Judging

ENTJs are outspoken, forthright, clear decision makers who are effortless leaders. Their world is filled with possibilities, and they can view tough situations as challenges to be resolved. They are goal oriented and constantly look for channels to turn challenging situations into solutions. ENTJs are inclined towards long-term plans and setting high goals. They are knowledgeable, informed, forceful and persuasive while presenting ideas. Though ENTJs aren't much attuned to other's feelings,they have a powerful sentimental side.

Determining Personality Type

The Myers-Briggs personality type was a personality assessment system founded by mother-daughter duo Katharine Cook Briggs and Isabel Briggs Myers. It was invented with the objective of helping women find jobs that were most suitable for their personalities when World War II commenced. The idea was just like one side of the brain is dominant in each person, which makes them either left or right handed, people are naturally inclined to think, feel and act in a specific manner. Each of us is in a sense comfortable of acting or behaving in a certain way, which determines our overall personality. Here are some tips for determining a person's personality type.

Is the Person an Introvert or Extrovert?

The first reading parameter when it comes to reading an individual's personality should be if the person is an introvert or extrovert.This isn't as much about how social a person is as about how he/she tends to feel, think and act. While solving a problem, do they reflect inward or look outward? Do they think more about themselves or other people? There's no right or wrong here. You are observing someone purely from the perspective of determining their personality, and no personality type is good or bad, right or wrong from a psycho-scientific angle.

People who look charged and energized around others or by social activities are likely extroverted by nature. They desire to be around other people and possibly have a large circle of acquaintances. Introverts, on the other hand, prefer spending time alone over socializing. These people generally have sharp minds and think rather than speak.

How does the Person Gather Information?

While reading or analyzing people, pay close attention to how people gather information. Do they do it through a sensory experience or intuition? People who sense are focused on cold, hard facts, while those who feel operate on their hunches and gut feeling. Sensors don't depend on their gut feeling until it backed by logic. They are more detail oriented and mindful of their needs. Rather than relying on flashes of gut feelings or guesswork, they depend on observations of clean facts.

Intuitive folks, on the other hand, are more at home with feelings, abstract ideas, and theories. They are spontaneous, instinctive and imaginative. They tend to live in a future that looks full of possibilities rather than merely existing in the present. Their thoughts are focused on patterns, links and insight flashes. They have trouble living in the now. Have you seen people being so consumed and focused on future ideas that they forget to eat. These are most likely the intuitive people.

How Does the Person Make Decisions?

Determine how the person makes their decision after gathering information while determining their personality. Do they rely on other people's perspective in a bid to take a balanced and agreeable decision that makes everyone happy? This is typically the sign of a feeling person. Conversely, if they make decisions primarily by relying on logic and analyzing facts, their decision-making demonstrates a thinking personality.

Feeling personality types are increasingly uncomfortable when confronted by conflict, while the thinking personality types accept it as a part of dealing with different types of people.

How Does the Person Relate to The Outside World?

The manner through which a person relates to the external world also establishes their personality type. Do they openly express their perceptions and judgments to other people? The judging type will offer people advice about how to make clear decisions and resolve matters.

They like to come up with practical solutions for problems and have a more problem resolution mindset. If someone likes to make plans, checklists, and complete things ahead of their given time frame, they most likely belong to the judging type. Perceiving types like to share their observations with everyone around, keeping their options open before making up their mind. They tend to wait and watch until they make a decision or commit.

Getting a person to take the MBTI test is a great way to understand his or her personality. However, in the absence of this test, you can use the above pointers to determine their personality. The results may or may not be conclusive, but combined with other techniques mentioned in the book;you may succeed in reading people fairly accurately.

No one MBTI personality is greater than the other. The personality type test attempts to identify a person's natural tendencies, not abilities. Analyze people from the perspective of what they tend to be rather than how they should be or how you want them to be.

Chapter Five: Reading People Through Their Words

People don't just use words randomly. Their choice of words is primarily guided by subconscious thoughts and feelings. There is also an underlying meaning to the words people use. For example, if someone says to you, "you are dating another rock star." What is the use of the word"another" here means is you just came out of a disastrous with a rockstar,and now you have foolishly started dating yet another one!

Notice how people say "yeah, no" a lot nowadays. It can be a signal of ambivalence. Similarly, when people say, "dude" or "bro," it can be a sign of showing solidarity with you. It can indicate friendship and a sense of loyalty that the person feels towards you. Start paying attention to the words people use to peep into their subconscious mind and read the right meaning of what they are trying to say.

Look For Adverbs and Adjectives

The human brain is nothing short of a superpower. It is unbelievably efficient when it comes to thinking, feeling and vocalizing thoughts. When people think, they tend to only use nouns and verbs. On the other hand, adverbs and adjectives are included while speaking to convert thoughts into the language of communication. The words that we add to describe a noun or action fascinatingly can reveal a lot about our thoughts, values,and personality.

Consider a basic sentence such as, "I jumped" which consists of a pronoun and verb. Now the words that you use to modify this sentence can reveal a lot about you. These modifications offer clues into the behavioral patterns and personality of the person.Word clues offer the power to make an educated guess about a person's character. In the above sentence, if I add the word fast, it indicates a sense of urgency.

The person can walk briskly because they are late for an appointment, and are conscious about being on time. This can reveal a disciplined and responsible attitude. They respect societal norms and strive to live up to other people's expectations. These people may make for good employees, Walking fast can also imply a real or imagined threat. People add descriptive words that are a direct reflection of their thoughts.

Another Award

If someone says, "they won another award,"it simply means that they have several awards under their belt. It may be a signal of an insecure personality that constantly feels the need to let people know that they've won earlier as well. The person may be suffering from a complex that makes them vocalize their accomplishments. This is an indicator that to develop a good rapport with the person, praise them for their achievements. It helps you recognize an area of vulnerability in the person.

Look for a mismatch in the person's selections of words and body language. For instance,if the person says they are glad or happy to meet you, while their body language is stiff and uncomfortable, something may not be right. Inconsistency in verbal and nonverbal clues can be easily spotted by a trained eye.

I Decided To Purchase That Model

The word 'decided' means that they have weighed several options before purchasing the model. Perhaps they struggled to come to a decision before purchasing. The behavior suggests that the person takes times to think things, and then makes a decision. They are less impulsive and more reflective. An impulsive and extrovert is more likely to say "I just purchased that." Even a word like "just" in this context means that this individual has bought a thing without giving it much thought.

Based on the word decided, a perceptive listener can develop a hypothesis that the person using it is more of an introvert. Introverts almost always think carefully before they make a decision. They will reflect upon every choice before making a firm decision.

Pushing an introvert to make an immediate decision is likely to elicit a "no" from them as they like to mull over their choices and aren't comfortable making instant decisions. Conversely, extroverts can be goaded to make a quick decision since they are comfortable making immediate decisions. Before selling or negotiating, determine whether the person is an introvert or extrovert.

I Did the Right Thing

In this context, right signifies that a person has faced plenty of moral and ethical dilemmas, and overcome some internal or external conflict to make the right decision. It indicates a strong character. It indicates the ability to make a right decision even in the face of challenges or opposing views.

The Object Description Test

The way a person describes even a simple object such as a bottle can tell how they perceive the world, feel and think. Determine the most commonly used cluster of words, which provide a basis for their personality. This linguistic method is known as meaning extraction.

The I Test

This is another test that helps you decode an individual's personality or behavior. At the beginning of the chapter, we discussed how excessive usage of the word "I" signifies self-centeredness or a large ego. You would think people in a powerful and authoritative position would use the word "I" more often. However, "I" is generally connected with lower power control. This seems unbelievable at first. However, when you look deeper into it, you realize that only people who are insecure about power and position feel the need to reinforce their false power through "I." There is a greater need to impress superiors, which makes the use of "I" prevalent. Do a small exercise. Read through all the emails you've received from people in a high position of authority. Now, look at the emails of people who've given instructions to or supervised. You'll clearly notice it is the latter that uses "I" more often.

For example, "Dear Mr. Smith, I was a student of your sociology class year. I have enjoyed your classes, and I've learned plenty from them. I got an email from you about research collaboration with you. I would love to work with you" Mr. Smith, on the other hand, will reply with a "That's wonderful news. This week will be slightly busy for me because of a prior scheduled trip. How about a meeting next Monday from 4 to 6? It will be great to catch up with you. Apart from being an indicator of lower power, greater self-consciousness (in some cases can also be a signal of depression).

In a study published in the Scientific Study of Literature, it was discovered that famous poets who committed suicide eventually used first-person pronouns in their works more often.

Reading Between the Lines

Sometimes what people leave unsaid also reveals a lot about what they are thinking or feeling. Notice how even something as seemingly flattering as "you are looking good today" irks us because we catch what's left unsaid. Am I looking good only today? What about other days?

Let us consider an example. You go to a popular restaurant in town for a scrumptious, lavish seven-course meal with your family. The waiter does his best to introduce every course and offer you details about the preparations to keep you interested and informed. When you are done with the entire meal, you ask for the check. The waiter brings you the checks and asks you if the food was good.

You nod and simply say "the soup was nice." The waiter doesn't look too pleased. You wonder why because,in your mind, you paid him a compliment.

However, on a subconscious level, he caught what you probably left unsaid. That everything was average, and only the soup was nice or worth mentioning! What you indirectly suggested was that the rest of the meal wasn't as good. Thus, while you communicate a lot through what you say, plenty is also conveyed through what you leave unsaid.

Speaking About Others

We have often heard quotes that suggest how what we speak about other people is a reflection about our personality. In a study by Peter Harms and Siminie Vazire published in the Journal of Personality and Social Psychology, it was revealed that asking participants to rate people in three negative and three positive aspects revealed a lot about their mental health, social personality, well-being, and their perception of others. It was discovered that an individual's tendency to view others in a flattering light was an indication of their own positive traits.

There was a strong link between perceiving others positively and possessing an enthusiastic, optimistic, courteous, emotionally steady and compassionate personality. Speaking flatteringly about others reveals how happy people are with their own lives. Similarly, people who use more negative words to describe others seem to view themselves in a poor light too.

There is a high correlation between using negative words to describe others and dissatisfaction, narcissism, low self-esteem and antisocial behavior. Individuals with a fundamentally negative personality or traits often tend to perceive others in a negative light. It may also indicate a mental health issue, unstable mind or personality disorder.

Talking about others

Haven't we all heard that all famous quote about how what we say about us reveals plenty about us?

In a study conducted by Peter Harms at the University of Nebraska, and Siminie Vazire at the Washington University in St. Louis (published in the Journal of Personality and Social Psychology) it was found that simply by asking a group of participants to rate negative and positive characteristics of three people helped researchers understand the each participant's mental health, overall well being, social attitude and the way they were perceived by others.

It was found that a person's tendency to see others in a more positive light was a reflection of his or her own positive personality traits. He or she viewed others pretty much with the same filters that he or she used for themselves. There was a strong co-relation between judging others in a positive light and being happy, enthusiastic, courteous, compassionate, emotionally stable and able themselves. Talking about other people is positive, encouraging words is a huge sign of how overall satisfied people are with their lives, and how they are viewed by other people around them.

Conversely, negative words used to describe others are highly linked with antisocial behavior, overall dissatisfaction with their life, narcissism, and a low sense of self-worth. People with predominantly negative traits tend to view and speak about others in a negative or unflattering manner. It can also be an indicator of personality disorders or mental health issues.

Chapter Six: Personality and Birth Order

A person's birth order can determine their personality to a large extent. It isn't just idle cocktail party talk but a dependable socio-psychological way of determining an individual's personality through the role they play within the family, and the family's overall dynamics. A person's birth order determines the role he or she fills during their childhood or adolescence.

The status quo we are given during our childhood eventually molds our primary personality, the way we perceive others, and the way we relate to them. Our early childhood experiences have a deep influence on our subconscious mind. This is exactly why children born in the same family (or brought up in the same environment) possess a drastically different personality.

There are many factors that in combination with the birth order can influence an individual's personality. These factors (parent's academic and professional accomplishments, social economic status, number of children in the family and more)are interwoven and cannot be viewed in isolation while analyzing people with their birth order.

Alfred Adler, who worked closely with Freud and Jung, proposed the theory of analyzing an individual through their birth order. He used it as a psychological technique to analyze the personality and behavior of his clients. It was Frank Sulloway who gave the theory a more modern application through his book, *Born to Rebel.*The book identified five fundamental traits such as extraversion, neuroticism, consciousness, agreeableness, and openness. He also stated that a person's birth order influences his personality more than his environment, which means two firstborns will have more than common that two children who belong to the same family.

Here are some insights into analyzing people's personality through their birth order.

First Borns

Firstborns are known to be high on leadership skills, responsibility,and ambition. Since they enjoy undivided attention from the parents for some time, they enjoy an edge over later-born siblings. Again, they learn to take the lead and care for their younger siblings. This makes them more responsible, disciplined and accountable by nature. They tend to develop protective skills and often focus on leading the path for others.

Similarly, if parents place plenty of expectations of their first child, the child may end up feeling unable to match up to these expectations. This may lead to a more underdeveloped personality, characterized by a constant need for approval, acceptance, reduced self-esteem, low confidence, and validation from others. They may grow up with a feeling that they can never be good enough for anyone or anything.

Firstborns are focused on their goals, and place a premium on achievements and professional success. The enjoy positions related to responsibility, authority,and leadership. There can also be a tendency to be a control freak, bossy, autocratic and dogmatic. Firstborn children develop dominant traits owing to their order in the sibling hierarchy. They are often physically stronger than their siblings, which makes them display a more dominant personality and disposition.

Firstborns generally score high on determination, conforming to rules and are known to be detail oriented.

Middle Borns

Middle borns, because they are juxtaposed between two siblings, often possess a more complex personality. They may not enjoy the rights of their older siblings or the special liberties of their younger sibling. This is why they are known to be good at negotiators, peacemakers,and diplomats. They often have a wide social circle to compensate for the lack of attention they receive at home.

Middle born individuals are social beings and operate with a deep sense peace, justice,and fairness. They tend to be faithful and family-oriented, and seldom betray the trust placed on them.

Their typical personality characteristics are adaptability, flexibility, diplomacy,and generosity. They are free spirited by disposition. Middle borns often excel at more than one skill.

Last Borns

The youngest child or the last born possess a charming, creative and risk-taking personality. There is an inclination to discover new ways to do things rather than towing set rules. They don't fancy traditions and conventions and look for different ways to do things.

Since parents often go through the experience of parenting a child/children before the youngest child, they tend to be more relaxed when it comes to discipline and rules. The youngest child is often more indulged and pampered, because parents are more financially well-off compared to the earlier children. This is why many of them develop a strong sense of self-entitlement or being privileged.

Since rules are more relaxed for last borns, they tend to be more rebellious and non-conformist by nature. They get used to receiving pampering and attention. They are free-spirited by nature and have a tendency to not go by the established rule (owing to leeway in rules), which makes them more creative and inventive by nature.

Some typical personality characteristics of last borns are empathy, high self-esteem, rebelliousness, creativity,and stubbornness. They demonstrate the need for constant attention and are often known to be extroverts/social beings. On the flip side, they can be manipulative and often know how to get people to do what they desire.

OnlyChild

Only children generally do not have to compete with other children at home, which makes them more self-centered. They also tend to spend plenty of time in solitary pursuits, which makes them more innovative and creative by nature. Only children look for different ways to stay busy and develop entertainment skills to keep themselves enthralled. They often turn out to be self-confident, self-assured, assertive, detail-oriented, perfectionists and expressive individuals.

Since they rarely compete with anyone for attention, they are used to being in control and getting things done their way.They find it tough to cope with situations where they don't have their way. Only borns often find it challenging to share the spotlight with other people. They often want to be the center of importance and attention. They often look up to the adults in the home as role models, which makes them perfectionists.

Conclusion

Thank you for downloading the book, How to Analyze People:*The Ultimate Guide to Human Psychology, Body Language, Personality Types and Reading People*

I genuinely hope it has given you a treasure trove of insights into analyzing people's personality through tried and tested strategies, proven subconscious techniques and several practical, actionable tips. These tips can be applied in setting from business to personal relationships to social settings.

Whether you want to figure out the personality of a potential business partner during a business association or the suitability of a prospective recruit for the given job or the compatibility quotient of a potential date, this book is a handy resource for helping you analyze others effectively. If there's one skill that translates into success in the modern world, it is the ability to analyze people.

This allows you to customize your message according to the personality of the other individual to achieve effective communication.

The next step is to use the book and implement it in your daily life in small, slow ways to start with. Start by noticing people at the airport or doctor's when you have more free time.

Finally, if you enjoyed reading the book, please take the time to share your views by posting a review on Amazon. It'd be highly appreciated!